Looking at Type Series

Looking at Type and Spirituality

by Sandra Krebs Hirsh and Jane A. G. Kise

D1472839

CAPT

CENTER FOR APPLICATIONS OF PSYCHOLOGICAL TYPE, INC.
GAINESVILLE, FLORIDA

Published by
Center for Applications of Psychological Type, Inc.
2815 NW 13th Street, Suite 401
Gainesville, FL 32609
(352) 375-0160

Looking at Type is a trademark of the Center for Applications of Psychological Type, Inc., Gainesville, FL.

CAPT, the CAPT logo, Center for Applications of Psychological Type are trademarks of Center for Applications of Psychological Type, Inc., Gaineville, FL.

Myers-Briggs Type Indicator and MBTI are registered trademarks of Consulting Psychologists Press, Inc., Palo Alto, CA.

Printed in the United States of America.
Second Printing

ISBN: 0-935652-30-2

Table of Contents

Foreword

The authors acknowledge that there are many expressions of spirituality and a variety of religious experiences. While we have tried our best not to minimize any of the differences or slight other per-spectives, we are well aware that our perceptions are entrenched in our Judeo-Christian upbringing and traditions.

One of the concessions we made for ease of writing was to refer to the higher power that seems bigger than the sum of humanity as God. While this may strike some as too Christian, we hope that you can substitute your own preferred phrasing as you read.

We encourage readers who have quotes, practices, or examples from other traditions to pass them along to us. We would enjoy enriching these pages with experiences that are different from our own.

Looking at
Psychological Type

*When you are rightly related to God, it is a life of
freedom and liberty and delight, you are God's will.*[1]

Finding a right relationship with the spiritual side of
our being is of increasing importance to many people.
Whether spirituality has long been a part of your life
or is a new topic for exploration, using the concepts
of psychological type to illuminate your pathways to
God can provide key insights and practical
applications. The union of psychological type and
spirituality is a natural one. In most dictionaries, *psyche*
(the root of the word psychology) is defined as
"soul". The soul is defined as the intangible part of
us, or our spirit. Thus to tap into our spiritual side
through the psyche is to combine two schools of
thought; both schools are about intangible concepts
made tangible by looking at their expression in our
everyday behavior.

No two human beings are alike, yet if you
carefully study human behavior, certain predictable
patterns emerge. Psychological type is one method of
describing these normal ways of being, lending a
framework to the common-sense knowledge you
already have—some people are more quiet than
others, some are more outgoing, some are more
logical, some are more planful, and so on.

Originally conceived by Carl G. Jung in his work
Psychological Types, Jung's theory states that human
behavior is far from random. Similarities and
differences among people can be much <u>more</u> easily
understood within the context of his approach. Jung's
theories were later expanded upon by Briggs and
Myers, creators of the Myers-Briggs Type Indicator®,
and many other writers. Today the MBTI® is one of
the most widely used psychological instruments for
self-awareness in the world.

[1]Oswald Chambers, *My Utmost for His Highest*, p.80.

Psychological type theory describes four pairs of preferences for
- How you are energized (Extraversion or Introversion)
- What you pay attention to (Sensing or Intuition)
- How you make decisions (Thinking or Feeling)
- How you go about your daily life (Judging or Perceiving)

The combinations of these eight preferences result in 16 psychological types, each with a natural, created way of being—each with its own distinctive approach to spirituality. No type's spirituality is better or worse than that of the others, just different.

What Psychological Type Is

Psychological type is a quick way of understanding yourself and others *in general, not in specifics;* it provides a straight-forward and affirming path to self-awareness. As you learn more about the preferences, you can decide for yourself which of those preferences and which of the resulting 16 types best describes you.

In general, psychological type also offers a *logical model* to explain some of the consistencies of human behavior. While there is an infinite variety of ways of being, understanding the patterns through the theory of type provides a way to improve communication, emphasize the value of diversity, identify potential areas of conflict, and use appropriate language for dealing with emotional or stressful issues.

Knowing your type provides you with a *special vocabulary* for talking about your unique gifts and those of others. Psychological type is a *dynamic theory,* not a static description of what you will always be. You can use type to explore strategies for growth and development. The purpose of this booklet is to help you use the concepts of psychological type to discover those spiritual practices that are most natural and enriching for you.

What Psychological Type is Not

- Psychological type is *not prescriptive*. It is a tool for describing recognizable distinctions among people.
- Psychological type is *not a pigeonhole*—human behavior is much too complex to be described through a single framework. In addition, there is infinite diversity among human beings and within each of the 16 psychological types. People with the same type will share some common characteristics, but each will have many unique characteristics of their own.
- Psychological type is *not deterministic*. While Jung believed that you are born a certain type (think of the differences in siblings you know!) you are also born with a free will which gives you latitude for your behavior. You also have your own particular life circumstances which shape the expression of your type.
- Psychological type offers little information about your *competencies*.
- Psychological type is *not an excuse* for certain behaviors nor for avoiding certain tasks.
- Psychological type is *not about putting barriers* in the way of your personal or spiritual growth.
- For this booklet, *type is a tool*, not an answer book, for understanding yourself and learning how to make your spiritual life more meaningful.

Looking at Spirituality

Our society embraces the material world. With so much attention given to material objects, needs and considerations, there is a tendency to discount the spiritual world of meaning and values. Yet many aspects of our existence cannot be explained by obvious, physical realities or mechanistic logic. For us, spirituality taps the intangible world, the pursuits and ideas that allow for meaning, purpose and wholeness in life. To be spiritual is to find a relationship with God. Growing spiritually means to respect the sacred part of ourselves and others. It also means that the spiritual path involves being open to the mystical in all of us, reaching an understanding of God and working towards conserving all of God's creation.

Setting out on a spiritual path is different from most other journeys. On the spiritual journey, others cannot set your goals or objectives; they typically come from within. The spiritual journey is never over; there are always new truths to learn, other practices to try, and times of sharing experiences with different people.

Our desire is to help you find ways of living out your inherent spirituality in a manner that is most authentic and congruent with *who you are*. Understanding your psychological type when combined with concepts of spirituality can become a tool to support your spiritual discovery or enrich your unique spiritual path.

However, psychological type is only one tool for viewing spirituality. The lens of type will focus differently depending on your past religious or spiritual experiences, your life story, and your current stage of life. Still, we believe that psychological type can benefit your spiritual search in two ways:

- By helping you focus on those spiritual activities and experiences that are most likely to capture your interest and be meaningful to you.
- By assisting you as you analyze and understand your reactions to events in your life, religious practices, or sacred experiences. Why certain aspects of your spiritual journey are so very easy or so very difficult is one of the questions we hope this booklet can help you answer.

Finding the "right" form of spirituality for you does not rule out struggles, tragedies, or dark nights of the soul, for these are a part of life itself and often spur growth. However, when you know your psychological type, you can place yourself where you can be more receptive to God—more responsive to what God has in mind for you.

Our Purpose

For us, there is a natural union between spirituality and the constructs of psychological type (the essence of which is understanding oneself and respecting the differences which exist among people). We hope to help you be comfortable with how you best seek God. Or, as a spiritual director and friend of ours stated, she hoped our booklet would enable you to find those grains of truth in a culture which provides few guidelines yet is full of religious institutions ready to provide you with too many! If you are already on a meaningful spiritual journey, knowing your type may point toward possible directions for revitalization. However, your own best spiritual path could be very different from those practices you have experienced up until now.

The Starting Point of Our Journey— Looking at Type and Spirituality

Because we are so familiar with psychological type and Jung's concepts of the conscious and the unconscious, we realize that we may unconsciously have a bias as we write about type and spirituality.

Sandra comes from a family that combined, but did not blend, two major religious traditions. With ENFP* preferences, a type that typically is open to possibilities for people and chafes at anything imposed in a heavy-handed way, Sandra sees herself using psychological type to help others become more self-aware and in the process find more options for their spiritual life. Sandra believes God works in us and through us in mysterious ways and that one's personal

*The preferences are explained later.

spiritual path is just that—personal as well as individually crafted with God.

Jane, with preferences for INFJ, finds that she as well as many others of her type, tends to view life in spiritual terms. For her, it is often easier to look at how God is working all around us than to stay in touch with current events. Because so much spiritual literature is written from the IN standpoint, emphasizing silent prayer, study, and meditation, Jane hopes that these pages can help others find the less-known paths to God that are more natural for them.

As NFs, we share a passion for helping others reach their full potential and hope that these pages might help you to find fulfillment in seeking or expanding your spiritual paths.

How to Use Looking at Type and Spirituality

If you are familiar with psychological type, you may be used to the preferences being introduced in a standard order: Extraversion-Introversion, Sensing-Intuition, Thinking-Feeling, and Judging-Perceiving. For this booklet we followed a different order. Once we help you identify your preferences (pages 11–16) we move to the pairing of Sensing and Intuition for clues as to how you might best find God—what we consider the start of any spiritual journey. We then turn to Thinking and Feeling to help you continue on that journey by finding ways to decide about your various perceptions of God. Sources of energy (Extraversion or Introversion) and the structure of your outward life (Judging or Perceiving) are last since they deal with the natural direction of your journey, outward or inward, and whether you seek a planful or spontaneous path.

To identify your psychological type

If you are using this booklet without the benefit of the MBTI, you can make an educated guess of your preferences by working through pages 11–16. Which of each of the preference pairs seems to fit you best?

Once you estimate your 4-letter type, refer to the summary chart on pages 15–16 for a quick look. Read through the page for your type (pages 32–63). If you are unsure about your preferences, read related pages (for example, ISTJ and ESTJ).

For spiritual direction

Review pages 17–18, How We Perceive God, as a starting point.

Review pages 19–20, How We Act Out Our Faith in God, to learn of ways to grow spiritually.

Review the type-specific suggestions for your type (pages 32–63).

Consider pages 21–23 for further ideas.

For group study

Review pages 25–27 on spirituality in community to understand the contributions and needs of each of the four functional groupings of psychological type.

For people in transition or newly aware of their own spirituality

Use pages 28–30 for information on type dynamics and development. Then follow the above suggestions.

Brief Descriptors for the Eight Preferences

Extraversion
Primary arena: external world, others
External happenings
Breadth
Discussion
Want to know community standards
Try, then consider
People and things
Interact with others
Activity
Offer thoughts freely

Introversion
Primary arena: inner world of ideas, self
Internal reflection
Depth
Introspection
Set own standards
Consider, then try
Thoughts and ideas
Concentrate
Quiet
Hold thoughts until perfected or clear

Sensing
Literal meanings
Pay attention to experience
Facts, precision
Focus on here and now
Master, then apply skills
Details
Trust five senses
Evidence first
Specific examples
Immediacy/concreteness

Intuition
Figurative meanings
Pay attention to imagination/insight
Theory, patterns
Focus on possibilities
Learn new skills, then innovate
Big picture
Trust inspirations/hunches
Impressions first
General concepts
Anticipation/vision

Thinking
Objectivity
Logic-centered
Justice, fairness
True/false view of issues
Search for principles
Critique first
Acknowledge differences
Head knowledge
Firm but fair
Convince by impartiality
Content of message

Feeling
Subjectivity
Values-centered
Mercy, humaneness
Person/situation view of issues
Search for values
Appreciate first
Acknowledge common ground
Heart knowledge
Compassionate
Convince through personal meaning
Impact of message

Judging
Controlled
Prefer to decide
Plan
One thing at a time
Energized at completion of task
Seek conclusions
Settled, orderly
Select the best thing, then experience it
End results
Goal-oriented

Perceiving
Spontaneous
Prefer to gather information
Adapt
Many things at the same time
Energized by starting multiple tasks
Seek options
In the moment
Experience it all, then select best thing
Process
Discovery-oriented

Preferences in Spiritual Practices

Extraversion—Experiencing God With Others

Talk and hear about matters of the soul

Engaging/spirited-led explorations of faith

Inquiry and learning through group study/devotions of spiritual material

Service through evangelism and outreach as expressions of faith

Listen to people's accounts of spiritual events

Interactive retreat

Engage others in worship experiences through singing/acting/dancing

Corporate prayer/sharing of gratitude, etc.

Variety in spiritual experiences

Consider the external world as the domain of the spirit

Introversion—Experiencing God Through Ideas

Study and read about matters of the soul

Contemplation as a means to explore faith

Inquiry and learning through one-to-one conversations/discussions of spiritual material

Service through reading, journaling, writing to bolster one's own and the faith of others

Meditate on spiritual events

Silent retreat

Join with others in worship experiences for enrichment through singing/acting/dancing

Private prayer of gratitude, etc.

Depth in spiritual experiences

Consider the inner world as the domain of the spirit

Sensing—Experiencing God Through the Concrete and Specific

Regular, sequential study of sacred texts

Tangible/factual examples of God's grace

Sacred objects for remembrance and example

Find proof of the divine in nature

Inquiry and learning through step-by-step methods for spiritual growth

Live the spiritual life in the here and now with promise of eternity

Methodical spiritual disciplines

Spur to spiritual growth: The real and the tangible give evidence of the unseen

Following traditional rituals or patterns of worship

Service through applying faith to practical works

Intuition—Experiencing God Through Paradox and Mystery

Poetic writing/creative imagery to explore sacred themes

Spiritual arenas that allow for use of the imagination

Sacred symbols for inspiration and growth

Use nature to connect spiritual themes and patterns

Inquiry and learning through synchronistic interaction between idea, person and learning

Live the spiritual life with a view toward eternity, incidentally in the here and now

Innovative spiritual disciplines

Spur to spiritual growth: Belief in the unseen gives reason to seek the real and the tangible

Designing new rituals or patterns of worship

Service through applying faith to areas that need inspiration

**Thinking—Experiencing God
Intellectually**

Take an intellectual approach to faith

Get in touch with universal principles to
guide one's faith

Search for truths in sacred texts

Skepticism precedes conviction

Debate and dialogue on matters of faith

Inquiry and learning through explanation of
logical questions concerning faith

Consider the pluses and minuses of spiritual
practices

Service comes by working to establish truth,
structures and mechanisms, and standards
of accountability

Identify with careers of intellectual "giants of
the faith"

Categories of faith, practice, etc.

**Feeling—Experiencing God
Wholeheartedly**

Take a personal approach to faith

Get in touch with personal values to guide
one's faith

Search for personal meaning in sacred texts

Concern for personal relationship between
God and people supports conviction

Discuss and persuade on matters of faith

Inquiry and learning through explanation of
motivations, inspirations and examples of
others

Consider the personal impact of spiritual
practices

Service comes by finding ways to be
involved with people and provide help to
others

Identify with personal lives of compassionate
"giants of the faith"

Commonalties of faith, practice, etc.

**Judging—Experiencing God Through
Discipline**

The beauty of spiritual *exercises*

Practice a daily spiritual routine

Find resources that can help organize one's
spiritual journey

Schedule specific times for devotional
practices

Service comes by setting time aside to deal
with the needs of others

Spirituality grows through acts of
will

Inquiry and learning comes through structured learning experiences (i.e., read 8
chapters in 8 weeks)

Spiritual practices that remind us of what we
should do

Enjoy knowing what comes next or what is
to be expected in spiritual practices

Move quickly to decide what is appropriate,
good/bad, right/wrong, valuable/not
valuable in matters of spirituality—may be
in danger of gathering information only to
substantiate judgments

**Perceiving—Experiencing God in the
Moment**

The beauty of spiritual *experiences*

Engage in various spiritual experiences as
they come along

Use available resources as need arises to
support a spontaneous spiritual journey

Combine devotional practices with other
aspects of life

Service comes by acting in the moment to
meet the needs of others

Spirituality grows through an increased
awareness of the divine

Inquiry and learning happens during "sacred
moments" (i.e., read when led to do so)

Spiritual practices that remind us of what we
are doing

Enjoy occasional surprises or departures from
what is customary in spiritual practices

Seek to gather as much information or
experience before deciding what is appropriate, good/bad, right/wrong, valuable/not
valuable in matters of spirituality—may be in
danger of being too open and not deciding

Values Associated with the Eight Preferences

Extraversion
Many relationships with others
Expression
Action/doing
Inclusion
Spoken word

Introversion
Deep relationships with a chosen few
Quiet
Solitude
Privacy
Written word

Sensing
Security
Simplicity
Practicality
Adaptation
Realism

Intuition
Originality
Complexity
Creativity
Innovation
Idealism

Thinking
Tough-mindedness
Skepticism
Competence
Problem-focused
Logic

Feeling
Tender-heartedness
Trust
Compassion
Person-focused
Harmony

Judging
Perseverance
Organization
Consistency
Industriousness
Planning

Perceiving
Adaptability
Flexibility
Surprise
Playfulness for renewal
Spontaneity

A Brief Look at the 16 Psychological Types[2]

ISTJs tend to be systematic, painstaking, thorough and hardworking. They honor their commitments, keeping track of specifics, following standard operating procedures (when they make sense) and get their work done on time. They are dependable, straightforward, and stable—the *"salt of the earth"* type.

ISFJs tend to be sympathetic, considerate, and conscientious to those in need of help. They value harmonious settings with well defined roles, responsibilities, and practical ways to be of service. Each person's welfare is important to them. They will dutifully pay attention to specific needs and organize things to meet them—the *"behind-the- scenes helper"* type.

INFJs tend to be insightful, understanding, and future-oriented. They enjoy dealing with complex people or values issues in a creative and independent way. INFJs seek work that mirrors their integrity, allows them to build on their inner ideals, and uses their inspirations for the common good or for peoples' welfare. They follow through and can be counted on—the *"oracle for people"* type.

INTJs tend to be strong individualists who seek new angles or novel, logical ways to look at things. They are visionaries who value intellectual and conceptual understanding. Because they see the future possibilities so readily, they are tireless and determined to develop their theories, ideas, and principles. They see how all the parts fit together and can create new paradigms—the *"designer of the future"* type.

ISTPs tend to be realists who use expediency and reasoning to find the logical way to get things done efficiently. They value clarity of thought, contribute quietly behind the scenes unless there is an extenuating circumstance—then they act quickly to come to the rescue. They are problem solvers who seek independence—the *"walking encyclopedia"* type.

INTPs tend to be questors for logical purity of thought who are motivated to ask questions to clarify and examine universal truths and principles. Intensely focused on areas that matter to them, INTPs appreciate elegance and effectiveness in the realm of the intangible. Independent problem solvers and mental model builders, INTPs relish the life of the mind—the *"blueprinters of ideas"* type.

INFPs tend to be inquisitive, gentle, creative, and deeply caring about the human condition or the common good. They seek to follow their ideals, remind others of what is important in life, and use humor and insight to make their points, INFPs struggle to make their inner vision of perfection real in their lives and in the lives of others—the *"Joan of Arc"* type.

ISFPs tend to be gentle, compassionate, and considerate. They are often modest and self-effacing in their service to others. They seek cooperative, harmonious and warm work and home environments. They care deeply about less fortunate people, animals, and living things. Their assistance is often providing the right atmosphere to please others' need for color, music, flowers, etc.— the *"St. Francis of Assisi"* type.

[2]Some of the information in this table was previously summarized in *LifeTypes* by Sandra Krebs Hirsh and Jean Kummerow, New York: Warner Books, 1989. The descriptors for each type were first introduced in *Work it Out: Clues to Solving People Problems at Work* by Sandra Krebs Hirsh with Jane A. G. Kise, Palo Alto, California: Davies Black Publishing, 1996. Fuller descriptions of the types in terms of the world of work can be found in *Work it Out*.

A Brief Look at the 16 Psychological Types

ESTPs tend to be action-oriented, outgoing, pragmatic, and resourceful. They like to be where the action is and where they can use their quick wit at just the right time to solve problems. They are to-the-point, lively, and efficient. Enjoying life each day, they help others participate fully in the here and now—the *"just do it"* type.

ENFPs tend to be enthusiastic, inspiring, and charismatic initiators of change who value exploring future possibilities for people's growth and development. Resourceful, energetic, and perceptive, ENFPs often anticipate what people will want in the future. They enjoy variety, newness, and flexibility—the *"spark that ignites the fire"* type.

ESTJs tend to be forceful, direct, and practical organizers who value task accomplishment and closure. They use logical analysis to guide their actions. They enjoy being in charge, directing others, and providing structure while monitoring their own and the group's commitments. They are decisive and systematic—the *"take charge"* type.

ENFJs tend to be lively and eager facilitators who seek to contribute and inspire others to work together toward the development of people or the institutions which serve them. Warm, talkative, interpersonally aware, caring and cooperative, ENFJs listen to aspirations, then organize, mobilize, and structure processes to meet these aspirations—the *"values spokesperson"* type.

ESFPs tend to be fun-loving, friendly, outgoing and exuberant. They are relationship-oriented and in touch with people's needs for encouragement, comfort, and inclusion. They are sympathetic and generous with their time and money. ESFPs engage others in enjoying life to its fullest. Practical and realistic, they are often where the action is—the *"everyone's friend"* type.

ENTPs tend to be highly independent innovators, improvisers, and change-masters. They value originality of expression, challenging ideas and norms, and developing effective strategies. ENTPs follow their hunches and jump into new, intriguing possibilities for systems and organizations. The call of adventure, allowing freedom of action, is characteristic of ENTPs—the *"classic entrepreneur"* type.

ENTJs tend to be active and direct organizers of processes, people, and plans. They are goal-directed, big-picture focused, and ardent problem-solvers, especially of large and complex issues. They enjoy providing structure, establishing parameters, and designing strategies to correct existing and future systems and models. ENTJs have high expectations, are persistent and value fairness—the *"grand-scale organizer"* type.

ESFJs tend to be organized, structured, and responsible in working toward their goals of meeting people's day-to-day needs. They are hard-working, outgoing types who enjoy managing others as they work together harmoniously to complete tasks in a timely fashion. ESFJs use tact and care to carry out their work—the *"server of humankind"* type.

Using Type Along Your Spiritual Journey

Sensing (S) and Intuition (N)— How We Perceive God

Perceiving, either through Sensing or Intuition, is about taking in information, how we discover our surroundings, and what we pay attention to. Jung describes these functions as "irrational" because they are not under our conscious control. Our perceiving is spontaneous and we do so through the lens of Sensing or Intuition. However, what we see is very different for Sensing types and Intuitive types. Sensing types pay attention to *what is,* while Intuitive types tend to focus on *what could be.* Thus a Sensing type might look at red roses and see the lush color, smell the special scent, touch the soft petals, and praise God. An Intuitive looking at the same flowers might remember the rose as a symbol of baptism and recall memories of holding a firstborn child, thereby moving away conceptually from the actual rose to associations or connections that the rose suggested.

Each of us is rooted in perceiving one way or the other, even if the preference is only slightly felt. While initial spiritual growth comes through our preferred way of gathering information (either Sensing or Intuition), continued spiritual and personal growth over our life span often comes through experiences of our less preferred way. Thus we may find at midlife or beyond that our spirituality is enhanced by practicing or experiencing life through our opposite function for a fresh perspective. The Intuitive might practice perceiving God directly through real-life experiences and the Sensing types might ponder what God has in store for them.

Sensors are drawn to the reality of God

- Sensing types frequently experience the Creator through the reality of Creation. By focusing on how God is with them now and can be understood through what they hear, see, touch, smell or taste, they show how much the enjoyment of this life is one of God's precious gifts. Beauty is often found in the simplicity of faith.

- Sensing types are attentive to the present, the joys and beauty of what is. *"Putting seeds into the ground, watching them sprout and flower, and watering and pruning them brings me closer to God because I see a tangible act of God's creation."* They see God at work in the ordinary context of daily life, finding role models or events that have actually occurred as reminders of God's love.

- Sensory aids to worship such as flowers, incense, or music may enrich spiritual experiences for Sensors. Repeating common or traditional prayers or litanies often helps them feel connected to what has been handed down from generation to generation.

- For Introverted Sensing types, prayer is frequently conversational, telling God one's worries and sorrows, often in a chronological fashion.

- For Extraverted Sensing types, prayer is often through action, less so through words. Pursuits that tap into nature or those that meet the needs of others are often ways they feel closest to God.

- Sensing types enjoy learning about the facts, history, and customs of their faith. They enjoy step-by-step teachings that stick to the point and help them to concretely live out their faith.

- Sensing balances Intuition by concentrating on reality, balancing the dreams of what could be with the certainties of what is.

Intuitives are drawn to the mystery of God

- Intuitive types are comfortable with the unseen and relish dreaming about the possibilities that God might have in store us. By focusing on how God can be understood through the imagination, they add hope and fresh insights as they anticipate the future. Beauty is often found in the complex patterns of faith.

- Intuitive types are attentive to inspirations, especially about the future. *"The incredible sunrise reminded me of the wealth God's gifts to us and how faith in God will bring light even in darkness."* They envision the plans God may have for themselves, others, and the universe, seeking potential for growth and change.

- Imaginative aids to worship such as guided imagery, symbols upon which to meditate, chances to be creative, or parables with underlying meanings often help Intuitives tap into the sacred in new or innovative ways.

- For Introverted Intuitive types, prayer is often musing with God about what could be different or might be in store for them.

- For Extraverted Intuitive types, prayer is often preferred when done in community with others. Their prayers tend to come from a desire to make things better for people, organizations, or the natural world.

- Intuitive types enjoy discovering the big meanings behind simple events or stories and then relaying their insights to others. They enjoy teachings that allow scope for the imagination.

- Intuition balances Sensing by adding new possibilities and genuine hope, not blind optimism, in times of bleak reality.

Thinking (T) and Feeling (F)—
How We Act Out Our Faith in God

The Judging preferences, either Thinking or Feeling, are about how we prefer to make our decisions. As we encounter God through our perceiving processes, we also need a way to effectively organize what we discover. These decisions—or judgments—are the province of Thinking and Feeling. Myers and Briggs, building on Jung's thoughts, describe the Judging processes as "rational" functions, exercised through our will in reaction to what we perceive. However, while both Thinking and Feeling are *rational,* the Thinking process is logical and the Feeling process is values-centered. One might call the Thinking spiritual path, the way of the mind, and the Feeling spiritual path, the way of the heart.

Some Thinking types assume that they have never had a "peak" experience with God because they tend to lack the spiritual highs and emotional grounding of Feeling types. Many Feeling types tend to struggle to objectively explain the existence of God or debate effectively the difference God's presence makes in their lives. At midlife or in times of transition, you might find your actions of faith enhanced by your opposite preference. For example, Thinking types may want to explore their values and their relationships with others while Feeling types may decide to revisit the logical underpinnings of their faith.

Thinking taps into God head-to-head

- Thinking types frequently experience God through their search for truth as they attempt to explain history as well as the events around them. Skepticism and distrust for the emotional aspects of faith lead them toward a more intellectual conviction of faith. Thinkers add an awareness of the principles which God has established for us.

- Thinking types are attentive to order, justice, and wisdom. *"God comes as I search to answer, 'Why?' I know I can wrestle with myself, others, or even with God, present the issues I see, and thereby move from doubt to faith."*

- Aids to worship need to engage the mind, either through clarity of teachings or the development of disciplines that demand the use of logic or reason. Sacred texts are examined for wisdom and truth.

- For Extraverted Thinking types, prayer might involve acting to change the structures that seem corrupt or unfair. They may see sin as untruths, dishonesty, or personal incongruity.

- For Introverted Thinking types, prayer often involves skepticism, confronting God on issues that involve ethics and principles.

- Thinking types often learn by asking the "big" questions, seeking intellectual challenge, studying the works of theologians, discussing paradoxes with other Thinking types, and using other disciplined approaches to acquire more knowledge about their faith.

- Thinking balances Feeling with a healthy questioning that can lead to greater understanding of the truths of faith.

Feeling taps into God heart-to-heart

- Feeling types frequently experience God through warmth and closeness to others or to ideals that lead them to a personal and intimate faith. By focusing on how God loves them, they add an awareness of the God who comforts, walks alongside, and rejoices with people.

- Feeling types are attentive to the joys, longings, and emotions of our spiritual journey. *"I may not understand why something has happened, but I feel God's presence. I know in my heart that God is alive in my life."*

- Aids to worship need to tap into the intra- and interpersonal aspects of faith, including stories or teachings that engage or are in line with personal values. Sacred texts are examined for personal meaning.

- For Extraverted Feeling types, prayer often involves acts of service for others as well as prayers with and for the needs of people and the community. They may see sin as insensitivity to or neglect of others.

- For Introverted Feeling types, prayer often involves sharing the sentiments of one's own heart as well as offering petitions for others.

- Feeling types often learn by celebrating common values with others, reflecting on universal goodness and beauty, imagining themselves as a character in a sacred text, or writing or listening to stories that engage their emotions or cause them to remember how God has personally touched them or other individuals or groups who are important to them.

- Feeling balances Thinking by emphasizing a God who wants to be in relationship with us and wants us in community with each other.

Extraversion (E) or Introversion (I)— Gaining Energy for Our Spiritual Journey

Depending on the approach you take, your spirituality may be a source of energy for your life or it may seem like one more burden in an already complex schedule—finding those practices that inspire and invigorate you spiritually makes all the difference. The experiences or atmospheres that energize us spiritually vary widely from person to person. One way for discovering a spiritual path that can rejuvenate your soul is to understand your preference for either Extraversion or Introversion.

Extraverts typically get energized when they extend themselves into their environment, seeking variety and outside stimulation. Introverts, on the other hand, usually defend themselves from the outside world because they are energized by all the activity inside their mind. Therefore Introverts often want time for private reflection and reprieve from the external world.

Picture an Extravert, who is generally energized by action and interaction with others, on a *silent* retreat or in a prayer service that includes long pauses for meditation. Such a person might mistakenly conclude, "Why can't I pray silently for long periods? I simply must not be very spiritual." Some Extraverts may even find it difficult to engage in spiritual practices when they are alone. Instead they see God reflected through their own actions and through the words of others.

Then imagine an Introvert, who is typically energized by the inner world of thoughts and ideas, on a workshop retreat filled with group discussions and active learning activities requiring lots of participation. Such a person might complain, "This isn't helping—I can't even articulate my questions because I haven't had time to process what we've experienced." Additionally, some Introverts may refrain from praying aloud even with close friends, preferring to pray privately.

Extraverts and Introverts can gain insight by learning and praying in ways that honor the opposite preference, but we need to first be in tune to the ways in which we best seek God. At midlife or at other times when you are seeking to reenergize, it may be helpful to engage in activities related more closely to those of your opposite preference. You may even find at midlife that your tolerance for different activities changes. For example, Extraverts may seek out solitude and quiet for their spiritual practices while Introverts may want to express and/or discuss their beliefs with others.

Extraverts Gain Energy by Meeting God in the World Around Them	Introverts Gain Energy by Meeting God in the World of Ideas
• Extraverts frequently encounter God through the people they meet or events they experience. They may seek situations where there is a lot of interaction.	• Introverts frequently experience God in moments of solitude. They may seek atmospheres where they can avoid interruptions and distractions.
• Extraverts prefer to talk through sacred practices and experiences in order to process what they are learning.	• Introverts prefer to introspect on sacred practices and experiences, using times of seclusion to process what they are learning.
• Oral teachings and the spoken word aid in absorbing new ideas. Often, Extraverts would rather sample a variety of spiritual topics rather than spend large amounts of time on one subject.	• Studying the written word, on their own or with one or two other people, aids in absorbing new ideas. Journaling may help to process spiritual concepts in depth.
• Use socially-oriented retreats for renewal.	• Use meditation-oriented retreats for renewal.
• Enjoy gathering with different groups that are perhaps loosely organized and then disbanded.	• Enjoy establishing a small, close group which stays together over time.
• Extraverts may express their spirituality by dynamic participation in action or service, reaching out often with many others in response to the needs they perceive.	• Introverts may express their spirituality through a few carefully selected tasks, often choosing to act or serve with people they know well.
• Extraversion balances Introversion by calling attention to the God who joins with us as we gather together.	• Introversion balances Extraversion by calling attention to the God who seeks to dwell within us.

Judging (J) or Perceiving (P)—How We Live Out Our Spirituality

The way we prefer to live our outside life—the one others see—often reflects our preference for Judging or Perceiving. This preference has a significant impact on our spiritual journey. Because Judging types like to plan their work and work their plan, they often tackle their spiritual life with the same sorts of goal-oriented schedules and structures that dictate their work habits. Those with a preference for Perceiving, who like to remain flexible and open to whatever turns up, often find that systematic spiritual disciplines (which permeate literature on prayer and other writings on enriching one's faith life) threaten to dampen their chances of finding the sacred as they go about experiencing life.

Judging—Spirituality Comes Through Regular Practice

- Judging types tend to schedule regular times to be in touch with the sacred in their lives. They may have made clear decisions about their exact beliefs.

- Judging types often prefer opportunities for spiritual growth that are defined—set study courses, prescribed times, exercises, or regular meetings with others to work toward mutual goals.

- Judging types are most at ease in worship experiences that follow a schedule. Many become uncomfortable if these experiences run well over their scheduled time because that could intrude on their other commitments.

- Judging types may use journaling, benchmarks, or other tools to mark their spiritual progress. *"Reviewing what I've studied up until now encourages me to stick to my spiritual goals for the rest of this year."*

- Judging types may be so committed to their plan of action for pursuing spiritual matters that they may lose openness to new paths that might prove enriching.

- Judging types may become frustrated with the ad-hoc spiritual practices of Perceiving types, not comprehending how spiritual growth can happen without discipline. When Judging types compartmentalize on spirituality too much, they may struggle to integrate faith with their everyday activities.

- Judging balances Perceiving by ensuring that the necessary rhythms of the spiritual journey, as well as those of a community of faith, are observed and continued with some degree of regularity.

Perceiving—Spirituality Comes Through Spontaneity

- Perceiving types tend to find the sacred in their everyday life, through serendipitous connections which reflect God. They may find it difficult to articulate their exact beliefs as they remain open to learning from new experiences.

- Perceiving types often find different opportunities for spiritual growth, often during the same time period, gaining energy by juggling various practices, and purposely avoiding any routine that might become stifling.

- Perceiving types may become engrossed in worship experiences, if they are enjoying them, unaware of the passing time and their other commitments.

- Realization of spiritual growth comes as more of a revelation. *"I was surprised when I noticed that spiritual situation more easily than I would have a year ago. The experiences of the past months have increased my understanding."*

- Perceiving types may be so intent on exploring the infinite ways to experience God that they fail to discern what disciplines and practices are most meaningful or logical for them.

- Perceiving types may become frustrated by the "oughts" and "shoulds" imposed on them by their spiritual communities. Sometimes Perceiving types may doubt their own spiritual sincerity when others comment on their lack of regularity in their spiritual disciplines.

- Perceiving balances Judging by adding re-*creation* and spontaneity to the orderly and structured disciplines of the spiritual journey and the life of a community of faith.

Spirituality in Community— Using the Four Functions to Foster Harmony and Meet the Needs of All

Up until now, we have emphasized each separate preference and the uniqueness it brings to your spiritual journey. Most people, though, also find enrichment through being part of a spiritual community. With sixteen psychological types, and an infinite variety of people within those types, meeting everyone's needs in community can indeed be a challenge. One method for simplifying this complexity is to divide the type table into the four combinations of Perceiving (Sensing or Intuition) and Judging (Thinking or Feeling). This results in the four functions of the type table, ST, SF, NF, and NT, as shown below:

ST	SF	NF	NT
ISTJ	ISFJ	INFJ	INTJ
ISTP	ISFP	INFP	INTP
ESTP	ESFP	ENFP	ENTP
ESTJ	ESFJ	ENFJ	ENTJ

Isabel Myers characterized the STs as practical and logical; the SFs as sympathetic and friendly; the NFs as enthusiastic and insightful; and the NTs as logical and ingenious. Each of these functional pairings has a specific way of contributing to the spiritual community and drawing closer to God.

One of the benefits of knowing these four functional pairings is to understand how the different combinations of gifts allow each of the pairings to contribute to the spiritual community in their *own* way. Unless we learn about each of the differing views regarding contribution, disputes can easily arise. For example, the NTs concern themselves with the theoretical or achievement-oriented tasks and offer up their strategies and structures to the spiritual community. They are quite different from the SFs, who are more interested in all of the specific, personal interactions, meeting the practical needs of individuals, and providing direct help as needed.

Similarly, the STs and NFs are often a source of irritation to each other. STs tend to be concerned with the here and now—traditions, costs, schedules, sticking with proven methods, and handling things logically. Contrast this with the idealistic NFs who are concerned with helping people grow and develop a rich and meaningful faith by visualizing changes that could benefit others or the community. The possible problems which emerge when the STs and NFs work together are obvious. One may not truly appreciate the gifts of the other.

Remember that each of the four functions has a God-given role to play in any community that seeks wholeness. By keeping the following points in mind, each of these four functions can be allowed to contribute to and participate in a spiritual community in the way their particular bent best allows:

	ST	SF	NF	NT
Contribute by:	• Grounding spiritual matters in reality	• Seeking cooperation and harmony	• Envisioning the potential for people	• Conceptualizing solutions to complex problems
	• Adding logic and common sense	• Compassionately meeting the needs of individuals—being the "hands of God"	• Adding creativity to communication	• Seeking excellence
	• Emphasizing the value of tradition	• Creating a welcoming and friendly atmosphere	• Nurturing the aspirations, ideals, and values of the entire community	• Developing models and using them for the community's long-range planning
Concentrate on:	• Applying spirituality to practical needs	• Showing devotion in tangible ways	• Inspiring others to stick to their ideals	• Defining the truth and acting on it
Are engaged by:	• Teaching that is step-by-step, practical, and includes facts and clear definitions	• Teaching that clearly shows the benefits to people in everyday life	• Teaching that appeals to the imagination and searches for the possibilities for people	• Teaching that challenges the intellect and standards of the faith
	• Liturgies that give a sense of tradition to the faith	• Settings that encourage warm relationships in the faith	• The poets, mystics, and sages that give expression to the faith	• Liturgies or studies that use tailored or logical structures to explain the complexities of the faith
	• Applying spiritual principles to everyday life	• Seeing the concrete examples of others, whether in person or through story	• Working toward values for society at large	• Discussing or debating well-presented expertise from those who have sought to answer "Why?" or "Why not?"
	• Defining community and corporate standards and developing a consistent list of do's and don'ts	• Attending to the details of spiritual celebrations or holidays	• Communicating creatively using methods (stories, poems, music) that touch the heart	• Applying ingenuity to solve the complex problems of spirituality
Aspire to:	• Fulfill obligations and duties	• Serve others individually	• Inspire others to live lives of meaning and integrity	• Create lasting, effective, long-range change
	• Keep faith honest and true to its rhetoric—show by example	• Build community where people are valued, nurtured, supported, and loved	• Help earth become more like heaven	• Shift the paradigms or explore the criteria and theories of faith

Type Dynamics and Your Lifetime Spiritual Journey

So far we have talked about each of the eight preferences individually, but Type is more than just stringing together four letters—the theory of type dynamics holds that the preferences interact with each other differently, depending on the exact combinations. This dynamic interaction of your preferences has special meaning for your lifetime spiritual journey. Each person has a dominant preference (#1), which focuses on either gathering information (Sensing or Intuition) or organizing that information (Thinking or Feeling). You can only have one boss—as long as you are busy gathering information (if your dominant function is Sensing or Intuition), your Thinking or Feeling function has to wait its turn to act on what you are gathering. And when you are ready to act, the information-gathering has to stop. If your dominant function is Thinking or Feeling, then you want to decide what you know, then gather information to support your conclusion.

If your dominant function is Thinking or Feeling, then you may spend more time *organizing* and less time *gathering* information before you reach a conclusion. While the auxiliary function, your #2 function, may not be as well developed, it serves as a balance to the dominant function because you need to both gather information (Sensing or Intuition) and decide about that information (Thinking or Feeling).

The following table shows the ranking of the functions for the 16 psychological types. If your dominant function (#1) is extraverted, as it is for all the types in the bottom two rows, your auxiliary (#2) will be introverted for balance. Similarly, if your dominant function is introverted, as it is for the top two rows, then your auxiliary will be extraverted for balance.

People use their dominant function in their favorite world—the outside world for Extraverts and the inner world for Introverts. For Sandra, with preferences for ENFP, this means that she verbalizes her Intuition, sharing ideas in order to process them. Sometimes it may sound as if a person with extraverted Intuition is constantly changing stances on

ISTJ	**ISFJ**	**INFJ**	**INTJ**
1. Sensing	1. Sensing	1. Intuition	1. Intuition
2. Thinking	2. Feeling	2. Feeling	2. Thinking
3. Feeling	3. Thinking	3. Thinking	3. Feeling
4. Intuition	4. Intuition	4. Sensing	4. Sensing
ISTP	**ISFP**	**INFP**	**INTP**
1. Thinking	1. Feeling	1. Feeling	1. Thinking
2. Sensing	2. Sensing	2. Intuition	2. Intuition
3. Intuition	3. Intuition	3. Sensing	3. Sensing
4. Feeling	4. Thinking	4. Thinking	4. Feeling
ESTP	**ESFP**	**ENFP**	**ENTP**
1. Sensing	1. Sensing	1. Intuition	1. Intuition
2. Thinking	2. Feeling	2. Feeling	2. Thinking
3. Feeling	3. Thinking	3. Thinking	3. Feeling
4. Intuition	4. Intuition	4. Sensing	4. Sensing
ESTJ	**ESFJ**	**ENFJ**	**ENTJ**
1. Thinking	1. Feeling	1. Feeling	1. Thinking
2. Sensing	2. Sensing	2. Intuition	2. Intuition
3. Intuition	3. Intuition	3. Sensing	3. Sensing
4. Feeling	4. Thinking	4. Thinking	4. Feeling

a subject, but in reality new ideas are simply being voiced. Each person's *auxiliary* function, then, is used in the opposite world. Sandra's Feeling function is introverted, meaning that Sandra needs some time away from other people to process her values judgements and to understand how she will choose to make selections amongst her many ideas.

Introverts who have Feeling as their dominant function may be very aware of what matters and the personal impact of a situation but will keep those judgments inside. What others will hear are their ideas and insights until a values decision is called for—then their Introverted Feeling judgments are heard. Either Sensing or Intuition would then be extraverted.

Even though they do not show up in your four-letter type code, you also use your third and fourth preferences. For most people, the third preference resides in the background, playing a less prominent role in what motivates or derails you.

The fourth function, the inferior function, is the least developed. When you are operating normally, this function is fairly hidden—a part of your unconscious. Your inferior function is difficult to use well and can often be the source of mistakes—those with inferior Sensing may have difficulty noticing details; those with inferior Intuition may struggle to envision future possibilities; those with inferior Thinking may have difficulty with objective analysis; and those with inferior Feeling may find it hard to guess how others might react to a decision.

However, the inferior function often plays a special role as you move toward midlife and seek to grow or enrich your life. Think about it—the first half of life is concerned with establishing your career or relationships. Typically, hopefully you are using your dominant and auxiliary functions to do so, working within your strengths. The second half of life is often concerned with finding meaning or seeking wholeness or completion of who you are. Then you may be attracted to those areas that are the province of your third or fourth functions. You may have paid little attention to these in the past.

Perhaps the ways you naturally seek God have gone stale or you seem to be in a dry spell on your spiritual path. Consider using your inferior function to discover fresh experiences. Try something manageable in scope, with small, simple steps that can be easily accomplished. In your quest for spiritual growth, the dominant and inferior functions might interact in the following ways:

If your dominant function is:

Sensing:
Concentrate on what can be verified—proof
of God in the world around you, in your life
and in those close to you.

Intuition:
Concentrate on the unseen God, the
possibilities of what God has in store for you
and others. Bring optimism and a sense of
the reality of the impossible.

Thinking:
Concentrate on the logic of faith, developing
your own system of belief and aiding in
the discovery of strengths and weaknesses
of spiritual and religious positions.

Feeling:
Concentrate on the difference God makes in
your own life and the lives of others; hoping
to deepen relationships and meet the needs
of others.

**In midlife you may explore your inferior
function:**

Intuition:
Begin to envision new possibilities for the
future and enjoy more imaginative or
mystical approaches to prayer or worship.

Sensing:
Begin to enjoy the gifts of the life God gives
us in the here and now, the joys of the
moment. May find traditional spiritual
practices more attractive and may notice
God in everyday circumstances.

Feeling:
Begin to focus on how faith molds your
values and become mindful of how you
might be of service. Time with others
becomes more important and prayer
springs more from personal needs. God is called
on for comfort, not just for explanations.

Thinking:
Begin to seek a logical foundation for your
faith, perhaps in order to explain it better to
others. May be more willing to acknowledge
flaws or inconsistencies in your faith without
feeling threatened.

ISTJ

Do your duty and leave the rest to heaven. (Pierre Corneile)

Finding Your Path

One Person's Spiritual Journey*

"As a child, I attended religious services and classes with my family. I experienced the traditional rituals and heard the stories of historical religious figures. Knowing that all these knowledgeable people before me believed in God enabled me to accept on faith the reality of a higher power. I believe that God is present and listens to my concerns.

"I feel closest to God when praying or when fulfilling my duties to others—my family, my coworkers, or those in need of help. Gathering with people in a worshipful setting allows me to forget for the moment all of my other responsibilities and concentrate on God for that short, precious time."

Others Might Help Me On My Journey By

- Offering lots of specific, real-life examples about spiritual matters, especially ones that appeal to my realistic and practical nature.
- Appreciating the necessity for details when bringing plans to fruition and assisting me in carrying them out, thereby lessening my responsibilities.
- Helping me to relax and laugh, keeping me focused on the big picture and the overall meaning of faith.
- Supporting my ideas or decisions, upholding me with their actions or prayers.

Common Stumbling Blocks

- Enjoying my traditions and therefore not wanting to change the status quo.
- Becoming rules-minded as I apply my spiritual principles, sometimes overlooking exceptional needs.
- Seeking to know all the nitty-gritty and in the process missing the "big picture".
- Doubting that I am truly worthwhile because I'm all too aware of my areas for self-improvement.

*While these anecdotes are compilations of stories of people of each type, they *may* not speak to your own unique expression of the journey experience.

Spirituality Is

- Learning to set aside all of the details of life in order to be present to God.
- Wanting to travel on a straight path despite all the forks in the road.
- Behaving responsibly toward others and honoring my commitments.
- Very private, deep and somewhat unexplainable.

Following Your Path

Paths for Renewal That May Feel Natural

- Doing arts and crafts projects which allow for self expression, for either practical or aesthetic purposes.
- Reading all the works of an author in a structured and organized way to ascertain the consistency and truthfulness of their point of view.
- Serving as a resource to others who are seeking a just and fair way to handle matters of faith and in this process clarifying my own analysis.
- Doing a values identification exercise or meditating on matters that are important to me to check if my life is congruent with those values.

Paths for Going Deeper

- Traveling with others to places which can be spiritually enriching and/or exploring those histories, customs or traditions of my faith for a more well-rounded perspective.
- Committing to corporate worship or a spiritual discussion group where I can enrich my faith and understanding. Making room in my life for organized religious activities allows me an opportunity to leave tasks behind and concentrate on spiritual matters.

Trap: Being so aware of my tasks that I forget to step back and appreciate that I am already worthy as I am, not only because of my deeds.

*Hold them in the highest regard in love
because of their work*
(1 THESSALONIANS 5:13)

ISTP

Trees and stones will teach you that which you can never learn from masters. (St. Bernard)

Finding Your Path

One Person's Spiritual Journey

"Spirituality doesn't exactly come naturally for me, at least not in the way most people think of it. While I prefer to believe that a higher power is in charge of the universe, my strongest rationale for that belief is that I don't like any of the alternative theories!

"I tend to feel restrained by structure in any part of my life, so God seems real to me in my unstructured moments—when I am outside in the real world, when I see a particularly moving film, or when I pray with my children at bedtime. My beliefs are straightforward and I don't want them to be clouded by teachings or meetings that are pointless. If I live by my principles and give my time to helping others, I am as spiritual as I need to be."

Others Might Help Me On My Journey By
- Giving tangible, in-the-moment help in times of need which demonstrates their spiritual commitment.
- Reminding me that people and social conditions will not necessarily be rational.
- Providing me with examples of their faith in action, bringing to me a new vantage point.
- Allowing me brief "time-out" periods from others and from my spiritual practices.

Common Stumbling Blocks
- Allowing spiritual life to be more incidental or accidental.
- Finding worship or emotional expressions of others awkward or even intimidating.
- Not factoring the needs of others into daily living.
- Trying to reduce everything to a logical formula.

Spirituality Is
- Letting my actions genuinely reflect my words.
- Having hope.
- Carrying through on my commitments, whether or not they make me personally happy.

- Deciding firmly what I believe, even though there may be no verifiable basis for some of those decisions.

Following Your Path

Paths for Renewal That May Feel Natural
- Finding the sacred in the everyday, using quiet places for prayer and reflection, perhaps in the midst of other pursuits.
- Meeting with a few trusted others to talk honestly about beliefs and doubts.
- Volunteering in tangible, practical ways to help those who need immediate and concrete help, leading the effort if no one else will.
- Escaping from the rules of formal spiritual practices, either as a time of renewal, or to define my own spiritual experiences.

Paths for Going Deeper
- Attending a workshop where I can explore my values and become aware of what matters most to me.
- Concentrating on finding areas of agreement, offering appreciation to those who have shown me kindness, and listening and reflecting with others about spiritual development.

Trap: Isolating myself from a spiritual community.

But whoever lives by the truth comes into the light so that it may be seen plainly that what s/he has done has been done through God.
(JOHN 3:21)

ESTP

It is impossible to live pleasurably without living wisely, well, and justly, and impossible to live wisely, well and justly without living pleasurably. (Epicurus)

Finding Your Path

One Person's Spiritual Journey

"The church I attended as a child did not make a great impression on me. I found God when I realized the difference faith made in some people I knew well and really admired. They didn't just talk about it—they acted on it.

"When I saw these people able to love others in a way I knew I didn't—and serve others joyfully—I became interested in learning more. Finding God in the structure of a church is difficult since I prefer variety in my spiritual practices. My best paths to God may not seem 'spiritual' to others—I know God exists when I can help others tangibly or talk with them about what makes faith real."

Others Might Help Me On My Journey By

- Talking openly about the difference faith has made in their lives and *showing* that difference by caring about me when the going is tough.
- Seeing the lighter side of a spiritual life.
- Withholding their judgments about what I should/should not do to be a spiritual person.
- Joining with me in celebrating/enjoying *today* as a gift from God.

Common Stumbling Blocks

- Questioning the reality of faith—finding it hard to take future promises seriously.
- Being skeptical about immortality.
- Overlooking spiritual life because of my focus on *real* life.
- Finding it hard to be patient and open in dry periods of faith.

Spirituality Is

- Trusting it will all work out in the end because God is in charge.
- Having a set of beliefs that helps me cope in the here and now.

- Making progress in showing my beliefs in the way that I live.
- Living life fully, appreciating God's gifts by actually using them or enjoying them.

Following Your Path

Paths for Renewal That May Feel Natural

- Finding others with similar avocational interests and joining with them on recreational outings where we occasionally discuss spiritual matters.
- Working with other people where I know that I *tangibly* make a difference and am not just one of a crowd.
- Setting aside time to be in nature, using these opportunities to consider the miracles and wonders of God's creations.
- Seeking informal settings for spiritual gatherings that include active, joyous participation. Formalities such as having to dress formally or to sit still through long prayers or lectures detract from my wanting to participate.

Paths for Going Deeper

- Disengaging at least once a year from the real world by going on a spiritual retreat. Structured retreats help me concentrate on my relationship with unseen realities.
- Meeting together with a group of people who seem genuine in their faith. Often my spiritual growth comes in the reality of being with so many believers.

Trap: Spending too much time in activities, too little time in reflection.

Therefore everyone who bears these words of mine and puts them into practice is like a wise man who built his house on the rock.
(MATTHEW 7:24)

ESTJ

*To be both a speaker of words and a doer of deeds.
(Homer)*

Finding Your Path

One Person's Spiritual Journey

"As a child I participated in my family's religious traditions but once I was out of the house, I saw no real need for spirituality. I was far too busy pursuing my educational and career goals. Later, at the urging of my spouse, I joined a church for the sake of our children so that they could make their own decisions about what they believed.

"Our spiritual community provides a social circle and an avenue for meaningful and important volunteer work. While I still question some of the details, the majority of the teachings make practical sense and work to link my family together. I also like that I'm surrounded by role models who practice what they preach in most aspects of their lives. When we join together for a cause, I realize that something bigger than each of us individually is at work—and that something is God."

Others Might Help Me On My Journey By

- Working together with me to accomplish what none of us could do on our own.
- Reminding me that the world cannot always be efficient and that something can be gained even in chaotic times.
- Persuading me personally to try a spiritual practice by outlining its practical applications for my situation.
- Describing moments when they were in awe by what God has done, thereby helping me to appreciate life's intangibles.

Common Stumbling Blocks

- Not wanting to be very adventuresome, staying stuck with my tried and true spiritual practices.
- Taking charge of situations or making decisions too readily, forgetting to look for spiritual guidance.
- Needing proof about spiritual matters, usually wanting more evidence than is possible.
- Being so practical and logical that I miss out on the intangible results of classes or experiences.

Spirituality Is

- A way of determining moral and ethical principles and teaching them to others.
- Something to fall back on in the turning points of life such as personal crises or natural disasters.
- Seeing the interconnectedness that exists among people, thus giving me a reason to believe and to see things in a wider context.
- Confidence and knowledge of God that results in action.

Following Your Path

Paths for Renewal That May Feel Natural

- Spearheading activities for the benefit of my community—building projects, disaster relief, food and clothing drives, coordinating volunteer efforts, etc.
- Enjoying the company of others and experiencing God through those interactions.
- Incorporating spiritual practices into everyday occurrences, i.e., reading the newspaper, exercising, or commuting.
- Participating in a structured study of spiritual matters where people gather for learning and camaraderie.

Paths for Going Deeper

- Engaging in a process to establish my own principles and goals for the meaning and purpose of my life.
- Studying the myth, symbolism, and mystery of my tradition to find new insights.

Trap: Forgetting to consciously pursue spiritual matters; getting caught up in either the fellowship or social action of my spiritual community.

> *Be diligent in these matters;*
> *give yourself wholly to them.*
> (1 TIMOTHY 4:15)

ISFJ

*The firm, the enduring, the simple, and the modest
are near to virtue. (Confudus)*

Finding Your Path

One Person's Spiritual Journey

"I don't think I really 'started' a spiritual journey; I
was on it from the day I was born. As a child, but
perhaps even more as an adult, I enjoyed organized
worship experiences. I felt a part of a larger family.
The things I learned about God provided structure
for the rest of my life. I seldom really struggled
against God or rebelled, but rather asked for more
understanding of why some people have to suffer so
much and why evil things happen in the world.

"More than the organized aspects of religion,
though, I find God in the lives of people around me.
Through their example, and then through my own
experiences, I gained an assurance that God stands
with me and works through me, enabling me to face
adversities without crumbling."

Others Might Help Me On My Journey By

- Letting me see their spiritual side which serves as a
  model, an encouragement, and rich, connecting
  experience to me.
- Offering to relieve me from some of the
  responsibilities I shoulder, since I find it hard to
  ask for assistance.
- Taking the time to study and discuss spiritual
  issues that are a source of concern to me.
- Showing that they care about me and others
  through their *actions,* not just their words.

Common Stumbling Blocks

- Becoming so concerned with alleviating the
  suffering of others that my own needs are left
  behind.
- Not seeing how all the details add up to become
  the overall plan.
- Disliking complex and philosophical topics not
  related to my practical spiritual interests.
- Filling time with "all that needs to be done,"
  sometimes neglecting my own spiritual desires.

Spirituality Is
- Using the wonder of what I can see, touch, hear, or feel, to strengthen my beliefs in areas that I have to take on faith.
- Helping others to follow their spiritual practices.
- Following the spiritual injunctions or duties of my faith.
- Looking to God for guidance for each day and beyond, believing that God, who sees the bigger picture, is with me no matter what unfolds.

Following Your Path

Paths for Renewal That May Feel Natural
- Studying spiritual matters that I can apply to my own life, i.e., prayer methods, spiritual practices of leaders, or parallels between biblical stories and modern-day situations.
- Being a part of a small, structured group for prayer, support, and meaningful discussion of spiritual matters. Organized studies or methodologies for prayer are often fulfilling.
- Cultivating close friendships with people who care for me and with whom I can partner on my spiritual journey.
- Participating in retreats, preferably in quiet, peaceful and beautiful places to refresh and *relax.*

Paths for Going Deeper
- Studying and experiencing other spiritual traditions by reading books or listening to recognized authorities who hold those beliefs to see if they match my own beliefs.
- Spending time in spiritual imaging or carefree daydreaming, perhaps using art, poetry, meditation, or music, to open up new possibilities for meaningful activities that I can add to my life.

Trap: Deferring too much to the wants of others and forgetting my own needs.

*Pursue righteousness, godliness, faith, love,
endurance, gentleness*
(1 Timothy 6:1, NRSV)

ISFP

*The greatest pleasure I know is to do a good deed by
stealth and have it found out by accident.
(Charles Lamb)*

Finding Your Path

One Person's Spiritual Journey

"My spirituality seemed to appear by osmosis. I was
convinced by the power of faith in the lives of people
I knew well. No other proof was needed—I just
believed. When a person I admired explained the
essentiality of her spiritual journey in a clean, clear,
and understandable way, it was easy for me to commit
even more deeply. I struggled, though, with the
organized part of religion, especially those rules and
regulations which defined who was spiritual and who
was not.

"To me, God is a personal friend whose tenderness
and love are real. All of this is intensely deep and
personal and therefore hard to explain in a way that
truly captures its essence. However, whether or not I
can describe my faith, I know God will stand close and
hold my hand through whatever life brings."

Others Might Help Me On My Journey By

- Allowing me to reach my own spiritual goals in
  my way, perhaps only providing a *gentle* structure
  for discipline.
- Offering warmth and emotional support in times
  of spiritual crises or change.
- Inviting and encouraging me to join with them in
  taking some risks, be they physical or
  interpersonal.
- Being appreciative of my quiet behind-the-scenes
  work.

Common Stumbling Blocks

- Devaluing my own talents and gifts when
  contributing to my spiritual community.
- Taking on too many good deeds for the welfare of
  others and overlooking my own needs in the
  process.
- Keeping my opinions on spiritual matters to
  myself *until* my values are crossed—then watch
  out!

- Not voicing how the actions of others have affected me, preferring to avoid disharmony.

Spirituality Is
- Being the hands and feet of God in the world.
- Living my life according to my values and beliefs as best I can.
- Trusting that God has my best interest in mind, even in bad times.
- Practicing devotion and humility in my own spiritual practices by not calling attention to my beliefs.

Following Your Path

Paths for Renewal That May Feel Natural
- Seeking private time at home, in a garden, or with pets or animals where I can enjoy the wonder of living things.
- Helping others learn about spiritual matters in simple, step-by-step terms that also allow me to internalize what I believe.
- Joining a small group of close friends for prayer and spiritually-focused conversation. Informal settings, perhaps in homes, with food and fellowship, make the gatherings more special.
- Learning opportunities that have a spiritual component, i.e., workshops or classes about parenting, getting organized, communication, marriage, etc.

Paths for Going Deeper
- Scheduling a lengthy time for solitude, either in nature or at a retreat center *or* considering a longer service opportunity where I can get to know others as we work together.
- Memorizing meaningful passages from sacred texts, enrolling in classes that focus on the historical or logical aspects of faith, or evaluating how formal doctrines fit with my personal values.

Trap: Going beyond my physical and/or emotional limits to be of service to others.

Truly I tell you, just as you did it to one of the least of these who are members of my family, you did it to me.
(MATTHEW 25:40, NRSV)

ESFP

To love what you do and feel that it matters—how could anything be more fun? (Katherine Graham)

Finding Your Path

One Person's Spiritual Journey

"My early religious experiences were a bit dry— the lectures and set prayers didn't do much for me, but I enjoyed being with my friends and also didn't want to disappoint my parents. I remember trying to tell a youth leader that I felt close to God when I was outside and could wonder about the magnitude of a being who could create such a world. Besides, being inside a formal religious setting made me restless. He thought such talk was irresponsible!

"Later, though, I searched on my own to find my answers to the big questions of life. I soon learned to seek answers as the need arose—I had too many questions to tackle all at once. I connected with a fellowship that made faith a part of their lives. We meet to study, but we also enjoy life together, be it celebrating a birth, skipping stones across a lake, or retreating together, enjoying fun and fellowship away from our normal routine."

Others Might Help Me On My Journey By

- Working with me to see what God might be doing *beyond* what I experience in the here and now.
- Helping me question what is best for me in given circumstances but allowing me to choose my own course of action.
- Joining with me in spiritual practices or journeys even though other delightful aspects of life beckon.
- Taking time to listen and talk with me one-to-one.

Common Stumbling Blocks

- Neglecting to make time for God and spirit-filled matters.
- Not giving enough thought to the future.
- Being too generous or giving too much of myself to others.
- Expecting my spiritual practices to be more organized and regular than I am naturally.

Spirituality Is
- Enjoying and appreciating what God has created; being thankful for all of our blessings.
- Assisting those who need help in a practical, direct way.
- Having confidence that God cares for me and that I'm on the right path.
- The essence of life—an added dimension to what we experience, filling our thoughts and actions with new richness.

Following Your Path

Paths for Renewal That May Feel Natural
- Participating with others in vibrant, joyful expressions of spirituality.
- Having time away with a congenial group for playful but spiritual activities such as camping, skiing, or sight-seeing.
- Visiting the sick and elderly, giving aid in emergencies, and tangibly experiencing God in these ways.
- Spending time in the company of trusted, close friends to talk about our faith journeys. Hearing about others' experiences, as well as reading biographies, to see and understand how God works.

Paths for Going Deeper
- Spending time in solitude, reflecting and journaling on the events and concerns in my life. A beautiful, natural setting often makes this easier.
- Going beyond my five senses to look at a situation and what it could mean in the larger context of life, what other possibilities there might be, and how it might relate to a non-physical dimension of life.

Trap: Trying to help everyone at the same time.

A cheerful heart is good medicine
(PROVERBS 17:22)

ESFJ

*After the verb "To Love," "To Help" is the most
beautiful verb in the world. (Bertha von Suttner)*

Finding Your Path

One Person's Spiritual Journey

"As a child I attended services at my parents' religious community, but I always thought of God as a rule maker and judge—I was certain I fell short. As I grew, I was hungry for a God that would offer me a secure source of love to help me feel whole and complete.

"I wanted an authentic relationship with God—I found it after I did my own assessment of right and wrong. Then I was able to order my life and enhance my spiritual practices. Now I feel that I have an outlet for my faith. The more uncertainties that life brings my way, the more comfort I find in knowing that God is there. I can't imagine my life without a close relationship to God."

Others Might Help Me On My Journey By

- Talking through spiritual issues and explaining to me the basis for their own life choices.
- Contributing their fair share and assuming some responsibility so I don't feel overburdened.
- Showing their love for me in concrete ways, especially when I am feeling undeserving or am in the midst of a crisis.
- Helping me remember to have faith when I feel concerned about the welfare of someone I love.

Common Stumbling Blocks

- Being driven by "should's"—aiming for perfection to meet my own standards or the standards of others.
- Sweeping conflicts under the rug to maintain harmony and to avoid being considered judgmental.
- Staying with the same spiritual practices, hesitating to try new or different ideas, even when the results of my current practices aren't satisfying.
- Being reluctant to question spiritual tradition or leaders.

Spirituality Is
- A conscious effort to look for God's presence in the actions of others.
- A rudder that is unshakable; a truth that stays when the storms of life come along.
- Loving God enough to actively pass that love on to others.
- Making time for daily or special spiritual rituals and traditions.

Following Your Path

Paths for Renewal That May Feel Natural
- Participating in organized studies or classes with groups that gather for fellowship in addition to learning.
- Defining for myself spiritual concepts such as love, unity, and truth, and what each means for my spiritual journey, by evaluating my own personal experiences and those of people I admire.
- Being involved in service or outreach programs that uplift or enable people to live better.
- Joining friends for long walks in natural surroundings or meeting in coffee houses or other intimate settings to discuss topics of faith and spirituality.

Paths for Going Deeper
- Using a logical framework to evaluate my spiritual development and to find those areas that need improvement, i.e., cause . . . effect, if . . . then.
- Engaging in academic course work and studying sacred texts or world religions to increase my world view and add to the richness of my faith.

Trap: Focusing on others first, forgetting to "analyze" what is truly important to me.

*For I am not seeking my own good but the good of
many, so that they may be saved*
(1 CORINTHIANS 10:33)

INFJ

The most beautiful thing we can experience is the mysterious. It is the source of all true art and science. (Einstein)

Finding Your Path

One Person's Spiritual Journey

"I can't remember not being aware of God—that a creator existed who cared for us was as believable to me as a child as anything I studied in science. Gathering with others to learn more about my faith was fun as well as very natural.

"However, as a teenager, I needed to prove to myself that God was real, not just accept what I'd been told. After extensive study, I found out just exactly what God meant to me. I then made a conscious decision to live my life for God. That means I live what I know to be true about God—and doing so is a treasure worth any price."

Others Might Help Me On My Journey By

- Understanding that I'm an independent and original person who often has a need to "go it alone" in matters of faith.
- Meeting in a small group in a disciplined way to encourage our spiritual growth.
- Sharing how they have deepened their faith so they can give to others.
- Allowing me the freedom to strive for what I envision and lending support while I do so, saying "Go for it, you can do it!"

Common Stumbling Blocks

- Finding it difficult to ask others for help, thinking I can work it out with God on my own.
- Reluctantly advocating for my ideas or talents.
- Focusing with such intensity on my own "vision" that I miss the suggestions of others.
- Withholding needed criticism to maintain harmony.

Spirituality Is

- Believing in and having a personal relationship with the Creator.
- Acknowledging that God is in charge and that there are some things I can't control.

- Trying to live a life of example so others might see good works and reflect upon God.
- Trusting and obeying the values and precepts of my faith—loving God and loving my neighbor in both word and deed.

Following Your Path

Paths for Renewal That May Feel Natural

- Joining or establishing a small group of committed people, setting goals for prayer, study, or fellowship and holding each other accountable to work toward those goals.
- Seeking study opportunities to explore in depth topics of faith that interest me. Studying sacred texts on my own to understand how the situations and precepts apply to my life.
- Practicing spiritual activities that actively engage the imagination—creative writing about sacred stories, listening to music which allows free reign for dreams and ideas, or keeping a faith diary.
- Considering all of life "sacred", looking for God at work in novels and newspapers, in the events of the day and in the people I know.

Paths for Going Deeper

- Paying attention to what God is doing *right now,* what I can see around me, what can I touch and hear; looking at God's wonders in the company of others, in beautiful surroundings or in small, practical acts of kindness.
- Finding opportunities to put my faith into action through hands-on service, missions opportunities and other authentic ways that might require sacrifice of time. This allows me to leave the world of ideas for the world of response.

Trap: Trying to work things out alone, being hesitant or afraid to ask others for help.

Therefore encourage one another and build each other up, just as in fact you are doing.
(1 Thessalonians 5:11)

INFP

*It is only with the heart that one can see rightly; what
is essential is invisible to the eye.
(Antoine de Saint-Exupéry)*

Finding Your Path

One Person's Spiritual Journey

"I can't exactly define when I became aware of God.
It has been more or less a part of my life since I can
remember. I have always been intrigued by the idea of
a spiritual presence and from an early age read books
about the lives of the saints, explored other faiths and
traditions, and appreciated poetry and music which
dealt with people's interactions with God and with
each other.

"While I did go through a period of teenage
rebellion, the outcome was a more personal and
deeply felt sense of *my* relationship with God. Now as
an adult I find God gives me a sense of inner peace
and is an anchor for my soul."

Others Might Help Me on My Journey By

- Telling me about their own deeply-held beliefs in
  an authentic fashion so that I can use them to
  reflect upon my own.
- Understanding that my spirituality is very private
  and personal to me, only to be discussed with an
  open and sympathetic person.
- Living out their values not necessarily with
  perfection but with true conviction.
- Offering me new challenges for an external
  expression of my vision and ideals.

Common Stumbling Blocks

- Taking negative feedback personally; shying away
  from anything but positive support.
- Believing that others do not *care* enough.
- Avoiding issues where conflict may emerge *unless*
  a value is crossed—then a tiger emerges!
- Coming across to others as idealistic and
  impractical.

Spirituality Is

- A wonderful and beautiful mystery never to be
  fully understood.

- Doing your best to live your life day-by-day in congruence with your values.
- Something very deep that transcends external spiritual practices.
- Being with friends and loved ones to share our spiritual journeys and practices.

Following Your Path

Paths for Spiritual Renewal That May Feel Natural

- Going on retreat for as long as possible to lovely, quiet settings to nurture my soul, engaging in journaling, poetic writing, solitude, and other introspective activities which explore values, the human condition or community.
- Reading and reflecting on biographies and auto-biographies of those who have led inspired lives or of those who have given much to others.
- Seeking out expressions of faith that involve beautiful music, drama, or other artistic involvement, either as a performer or as part of an audience.
- Understanding and feeling the needs of those who are in pain and anguish and ministering to them.

Paths for Going Deeper

- Taking a direct leadership role in areas that have an impact on my values.
- Investing time in academic course work about the theology of my faith, perhaps even using this training avocationally, if not vocationally.

Trap: Being entrenched in my ideals.

*Do not conform any longer to the pattern of this world,
but be transformed by the renewing of your mind.*
(ROMANS 12:2)

ENFP

The future belongs to those who believe in the beauty of their dreams. (Eleanor Roosevelt)

Finding Your Path

One Person's Spiritual Journey

"I don't remember not being aware of God. Hearing the stories of faith and reading accounts of missionaries engaged my imagination and connected me with unseen realities.

"I often sought intense involvement—not out of duty, but as a pathway to joy. Even as a child, I tried to marshal the help of others for my causes, raising money for animal shelters and disabled children.

"The hurdle was the regularity of my spiritual practices, although I've always prayed and stayed in touch spiritually. For me, concentrated periods of spiritual involvement seem to be followed by periods of more secular emphasis."

Others Might Help Me On My Journey By

- Allowing for doubt and ambiguity. God seems absent when rules or judgments are too heavy handed.
- Helping me to concentrate on the meaning of faith in its *daily* application.
- Sharing their deeply held spiritual values and moments of grace. Acting as "family", showing care and concern in times of crisis.
- Forcing me to slow down and pay attention to my spiritual and physical needs.

Common Stumbling Blocks

- Losing sight of spirituality in the preoccupation with activities and ideas.
- Neglecting to give attention to my own personal, physical, and emotional needs.
- Being so intrigued by all of the aspects of my faith that I jump from subject to subject, missing chances for depth.
- Going at such breakneck speed that I seldom give as much time as I want to contemplation.

Spirituality Is

- The certainty that God has a plan.

- A triumph of the needs of people over the dictates of law.
- At the forefront when I feel grateful, confused, or in need of help.
- Knowing in my bones that there is a God—"Only believe and all things are possible, only believe."

Following Your Path

Paths for Renewal That May Feel Natural
- Gathering with like-minded people in spiritual discovery and community where there is ample opportunity for discussion.
- Reading, talking, envisioning about God and spiritual matters from a wide variety of resources and traditions, both secular and spiritual.
- Enjoying the discovery of God in the beauty of art, literature, music, or in small acts of kindness.
- Leading or assisting people in spiritual endeavors that can help them grow.

Paths for Going Deeper
- Allowing ample quiet time for reflection in peaceful, beautiful settings that stimulate my senses, knowing that solitary times and retreats allow God to touch me in new ways.
- Engaging in spiritual discussions with "doubters" or those who hold opposing beliefs. In hearing and responding to their questions, I can discern more specifically who and what I believe.

Trap: Being attracted to the newest, latest, most attractive spiritual experience, movement, or leader.

Whatever is true, whatever is noble, whatever is right, whatever is pure, whatever is lovely, whatever is admirable—if anything is excellent or praiseworthy—think about such things.
(PHILIPPIANS 4:8)

ENFJ

*The heart benevolent and kind most resembles God.
(Robert Burns)*

Finding Your Path

One Person's Spiritual Journey

"In many ways, I took my faith for granted and wondered about some of my friends who seemed to need "aha" experiences or logical proof. I related to God as one would relate to a loving, understanding, encouraging parent.

"Recently, I joined a group that emphasized how God wanted a *personal* relationship with each of us, no matter what our spiritual experiences might have been. This insight gave me peace and assurance that God loves me wherever I am on my spiritual journey.

"As I worship and pray with other people, or more often alone as I grow older, I now feel deeply the presence of God and can rejoice in thankfulness about God's grace and faithfulness to me."

Others Might Help Me On My Journey By

- Encouraging me to consider myself and my own needs and wants.
- Gently confronting me, especially when I insist on everyone getting along, with the truth that even the best of relationships can grow as a result of conflict.
- Giving me permission to develop imaginative and creative ways for people's spiritual growth and development.
- Providing a personal and caring environment. When there is heavy judgment, criticism, or a sense of being devalued, I accomplish less.

Common Stumbling Blocks

- Becoming too emotionally involved in the success or failure of the spiritual endeavors I lead.
- Not having adequate patience.
- Assuming my way may be the most noble or altruistic.
- Taking the weight of the world on my shoulders.

Spirituality Is

- A natural part of life.

- Having an evolving, continuing, growing, and committed personal relationship with God.
- A vehicle to improve relationships among people.
- Influencing the welfare of individuals and the community; working with God to transform the world.

Following Your Path

Paths for Renewal That May Feel Natural
- Leading and/or organizing spiritual retreats which involve interaction, as well as time for meditation on specific readings or concerns for the well being of others.
- Spiritual discussions where I can build relationships, feel safe, and share my hopes and concerns.
- Seeking directed, reflective times for "being" with God and others in a connecting way.
- Developing new ways of helping others to realize their potential.

Paths for Going Deeper
- Attending academic courses, alone or with a friend, to discover fresh interpretations which draw out new possibilities for the logical underpinnings of my beliefs.
- Considering the pluses and minuses of my spiritual commitments to discover new insights/truths about myself and my spiritual journey.

Trap: Avoiding any expressions of negative feelings out of fear of disharmony—even in my relationship with God.

"For I know the plans I have for you," says the Lord,
"plans to prosper you and not to harm you,
plans to give you hope and a future."
(JEREMIAH 29:11)

INTJ

Nothing in life is to be feared. It is only to be understood. (Madame Curie)

Finding Your Path

One Person's Spiritual Journey

"As a young adult, I fell away from organized religion because I saw so many people filling the services who never actually *served* God. Their faith wasn't believable.

"God became real for me when I went through a personal crisis and had to admit there was an area of my life over which I had no control—whether I was fertile and could have my own children. This personal turmoil forced me to introspect about what or who should control my life. I finally admitted that I could rely on a power beyond myself. At that time I joined a community of faith where I found solace and could also be part of the solution to the many problems our society faces."

Others Might Help Me On My Journey By
- Being willing to admit their own doubts and intellectually explore the possible truths of our faith.
- Accepting that a cognitive approach to God is valid.
- Sharing stories of how they found guidance from God.
- Asking about my ideas and dreams for the future, listening, and granting me independence of thought and approach.

Common Stumbling Blocks
- Being reluctant to share my innermost self with others.
- Wanting to find answers to everything that interests or concerns me.
- Not feeling as competent as I'd like, perhaps trying to be spiritual, pray, etc., "perfectly".
- Expecting others to "see" the future and other complex spiritual issues as I do.

Spirituality Is
- Determining a moral base, a belief system of what is right and wrong, then applying it to all aspects of life.

- Being accountable to act for purposes bigger than ourselves.
- A consistent, deliberate, intentional relationship with God.
- Actively dialoguing with God about possibilities for the future and how to challenge society to take advantage of them.

Following Your Path

Paths for Renewal That May Feel Natural

- Seeking opportunities for solitude, such as silent retreats, to provide space for introspection, especially in locations that offer natural settings for meditation or walks.
- Getting involved in a project that requires me to learn or research a subject in depth, i.e., teaching or revising worship practices.
- Setting aside time on a regular basis (weekly if not daily) for prayer, study, or journaling; selecting a time and place with little chance for interruption.
- Looking for opportunities for corporate worship that involve purposeful liturgies that are unique and engaging.

Paths for Going Deeper

- Joining a team that wants to accomplish something significant, working not only on conceptualizing what might be done but in the hands-on implementation of the ideas.
- Observing in the here and now the little things which escape my attention that could enrich my life.

Trap: Being lost in thought and therefore not mindful of others or the situation.

*I devoted myself to study and to explore by wisdom
all that is done under heaven.*
(ECCLESIATES 1:13)

INTP

The first key to wisdom is assiduous and frequent questioning . . . for by doubting we come to inquiry, and by inquiry we arrive at truth. (PeterAbelard)

Finding Your Path

One Person's Spiritual Journey

"I think I'll be on a quest for spiritual truth my entire life. While I still haven't made a commitment to any one expression of beliefs, I've probably read more and studied more about spiritual matters than a lot of the people who populate churches and synagogues every week! I find it intriguing to examine different religions' traditions, looking for similarities and contradictions among them.

"Through all of this study, I came to a good understanding of the principles by which I want to live. However, my need to prove/disprove everything keeps my beliefs quite intellectual. One of the ways I've made my spirituality more personal is that each day I try to think of something good that has happened. This simple act of consciousness has helped me to analyze happenings through my feelings as well as my head. It's as if I give myself permission to feel spiritual."

Others Might Help Me On My Journey By

- Realizing that my questioning your beliefs is not meant to be critical but means that I'm open to being influenced.
- Presenting well-reasoned and objective analyses of their beliefs in a manner that shows they understand my point of view.
- Understanding that I do have feelings and emotional reactions, but that these are deeply guarded and therefore may be startling to others.
- Stating their insights and conclusions clearly and briefly, getting to the essence of the matter.

Common Stumbling Blocks

- Getting too caught up in skepticism.
- Intellectualizing and being mindful of "the head" while overlooking "the heart".
- Underestimating the personal needs of others, at times overriding their concerns.

- Internalizing my spiritual thinking or journey to such a degree that I find little reason to act directly in the real world.

Spirituality Is
- Doubting the existence of God, then using those doubts to spur spiritual inquiry.
- Setting up logical principles and steps to prove the existence of God.
- Finding and searching for truth and fairness in one's spiritual beliefs and practices.
- Discovering an explanation for those things which do not meet logical criteria.

Following Your Path

Paths for Renewal That May Feel Natural
- Reading, researching, debating, and other intellectual pursuits to analyze belief systems.
- Attending conferences or taking academic course work related to spiritual matters.
- Developing overall models which help conceptualize spiritual life in a rational and orderly way.
- Reading and collecting books on prayer, mysticism, etc., for cognitive understanding rather than real-life application.

Paths for Going Deeper
- Participating in spiritual retreats which focus on self awareness, the interpersonal aspects of faith, or an analysis of key values.
- Finding concrete and specific ways to let others know I care or to let others know about me from an emotional/affective viewpoint.

Trap: Not realizing how my words are coming across, especially when I am in pursuit of truth.

And this is my prayer: that your love may abound more and more in knowledge and depth of insight.
(PHILIPPIANS 1:9)

ENTP

It is not in the still calm of life, or in the repose of a pacific station, that great characters are formed . . . Great necessities call out great virtues.
(Abigail Adams)

Finding Your Path

One Person's Spiritual Journey

"I've always been a self-starter—a person with a great deal of initiative. As a young adult, I was a bit skeptical of people who believed in God. To me they seemed naïve, but at the same time I envied their ability to not care what others thought about their views. I certainly didn't enjoy anyone questioning my thought processes! Besides, I believed in my own competencies and ability to care for myself and those closest to me.

"Eventually, I experienced a crisis where I could not influence the outcome. I began to search for something outside of myself to give me the strength to carry on. For me, that strength came from recognizing that there is something bigger than human effort can achieve, a God or higher power that understands what we cannot comprehend. My heightened spiritual awareness provides peace and a foundation from which I can charge ahead again."

Others Might Help Me On My Journey By

- Not overselling the benefits of a spiritual life; let me come at it on my own terms.
- Reminding me that I did my best and that effort, not perfection, is sometimes the better yardstick.
- Engaging me in a relationship that is thoughtful enough for us to share our problems.
- Sustaining my faith by sharing stories of people who experienced serious problems and survived.

Common Stumbling Blocks

- Taking on so many competing projects that I am pulled away from spiritual things—no spiritual routines.
- Relying too much on my own abilities, forgetting that I can call on God.
- Continuously gathering information on different spiritual traditions/practices, but seldom putting them into practice.

- Wanting to be as "expert" on spiritual matters as in any other area of my life, therefore being reluctant to voice any opinions on the subject.

Spirituality Is
- A wellspring of hope and freedom that goes beyond my comprehension.
- Often acknowledged or accepted after a period of pain and uncertainty.
- An ongoing process of learning to look outside myself for strength.
- Acknowledging that something bigger than me is in charge.

Following Your Path

Paths for Renewal That May Feel Natural
- Participating with others in exciting and rich experiences that celebrate our spirituality.
- Exploring more about spirituality by reading or tracking down key principles and practices about my faith and that of others.
- Gathering with a group of like-minded people to talk about big issues and other concerns.
- Being involved in projects, perhaps cross-cultural or even international, that better the quality of life for others.

Paths for Going Deeper
- Retracing the spiritual experiences of my childhood and the places where my faith was enriched, reflecting on those memories for more understanding of who I am today.
- Dedicating time for spiritual practices that I've learned about in order to determine their effectiveness for me.

Trap: Competitiveness with myself and others.

Not that I have already obtained this or have already reached the goal; but I press on to make it my own, because Christ Jesus has made me his own.
(PHILIPPIANS 3:12, NRSV)

ENTJ

Be not angry that you cannot make others as you wish them to be, since you cannot make yourself as you wish to be. (Thomas á Kempis)

Finding Your Path

One Person's Spiritual Journey

"I didn't set out to search for God—I was looking for ways to add meaning and purpose to my life. However, the more I made inquiries regarding the spiritual side of my nature, the more I was led to acknowledge that there has to be something with energy and intellect beyond human existence—God.

"Developing my own guiding purpose provides me with a directional signal that tells me whether I am doing work that matters. My spirituality offers me insight on issues I face, but with all of the tasks I am called on to do, setting aside specific time for God can be hard. To me, the spiritual side of life is meaningful only if we commit to using it to improve our world."

Others Might Help Me On My Journey By

- Offering opportunities to slow down and "waste time" on social interactions.
- Joining with me to challenge traditional thoughts, dogmas, and paradigms.
- Recognizing that for me, faith is more logical than emotional.
- Understanding that faith is a very personal thing and I therefore seldom look to others for help in this area.

Common Stumbling Blocks

- Not taking time to build relationships or consider my spiritual journey in my quest to be effective.
- Wanting to reduce everything to a logical formula or principle.
- Applying rigorous standards to myself and others.
- Wanting clarity about things that may not ultimately be clear.

Spirituality Is

- Commitment to a particular way of being.
- Belief in the interconnectedness of all things.
- A part of deciding what is fair and unfair based on universal truths.

- Knowing that I have accomplished something that matters in my life.

Following Your Path

Paths for Renewal That May Feel Natural
- Studying rigorously, debating and discussing with others in order to clarify the principles of my faith.
- Applying my standards by planning and leading work projects for various social issues or outreaches.
- Reading journals with the latest findings and advances in science to find patterns, insights, or ideas that aid in "cracking the code" of our existence in a way that strengthens my belief in something beyond concrete experience.
- Finding a place of grandeur for renewal or worship such as a gothic cathedral or a mature oak woods that points to the majesty of a higher being.

Paths for Going Deeper
- Participating in practical outreach work that involves one-to-one contact, listening to the needs and feelings of those who require direct help.
- Completing a values clarification exercise to lessen the seeming arbitrariness of my emotions and interpersonal needs. Meditating and reflecting to tap into my deepest spiritual longings.

Trap: Becoming too reliant on my own abilities, forgetting that I can benefit from the experiences and thoughts of others.

*Dear children, let us not love with words or tongue,
but with actions and in truth.*
(1 JOHN 3:18)

Further Resources

There are a number of good resources for further information on psychological type and the application of psychological type to spirituality.

From Image to Likeness: A Jungian Path in the Gospel Journey by W. Harold Grant, Magdala Thompson, and Thomas E. Clarke. Ramsey, NJ: Paulist Press, 1983.

Four Spiritualities: Expressions of Self, Expressions of Spirit: A Psychology of Contemporary Spiritual Choice by Peter Tufts Richardson. Palo Alto, CA: Davies-Black Publishing, 1996.

God's Gifted People: Discovering and Using Your Spiritual and Personal Gifts by Gary L. Harbaugh. Minneapolis, MN: Augsburg Publishing House, 1988.

How We Belong, Fight, and Pray: The MBTI as a Key to Congregational Dynamics by Lloyd Edwards. Washington, DC: The Alban Institute, 1993.

Looking at Type: The Fundamentals by Charles R. Martin. Gainesville, FL: Center for Applications of Psychological Type, 1997.

Invitation to a Journey: A Road Map for Spiritual Formation by M. Robert Mulholland, Jr. Downers Grove, IL: InterVarsity Press, 1993.

LifeKeys: Discovering Who You Are, Why You're Here, and What You Do Best by Jane A. G. Kise, David Stark, and Sandra Krebs Hirsh. Minneapolis, MN: Bethany House Publishers, 1996.

Pastor as Person: Maintaining Personal Integrity in the Choices and Challenges of Ministry by Gary L. Harbaugh. Minneapolis, MN: Augsburg Publishing House, 1984.

Personality Type and Religious Leadership by Roy M. Oswald and Otto Kroeger. Washington, DC: The Alban Institute, 1988.

Pray Your Way: Your Personality and God by Bruce Duncan. London: Daron, Longman and Todd Ltd., 1993.

Prayer and Temperament: Different Prayer Forms for Different Personality Types by Chester P. Michael and Marie C. Norrisey. Charlottesville, VA: The Open Door, Inc., 1991.

SoulTypes: Finding the Spiritual Path That Is Right for You by Sandra Krebs Hirsh and Jane A. G. Kise. New York, NY: Hyperion Books, Summer, 1998.

Your Personality and the Spiritual Life by Reginald C. Johnson. Colorado Springs, CO: Chariot Victor Publishing, 1995.

Background Notes

About the Publisher

The Center for Applications of Psychological Type, Inc. (CAPT) was established in the summer of 1975 with two major goals: to help make what is already known about psychological types useful in practical ways and to create new knowledge. Its founders, Isabel Briggs Myers and Mary H. McCaulley, adopted "the constructive use of differences" as the motto for this non-profit organization.

CAPT educates the public and professionals to view differences constructively by maintaining a number of services for use in education, counseling, organizational development, religious life, and research.

- CAPT houses the Isabel Briggs Myers Memorial Library, the largest collection of MBTI publications, dissertations, and theses in the world. Research services are also available through the Library.
- CAPT publishes and distributes papers and books related to research and practical applications of the Indicator. On-going research is conducted and made available through new products and services.
- CAPT computer scoring for the MBTI produces high-quality, professional reports. This service attracts a large number of MBTI users; it also facilitates the collection of MBTI responses, contributing significantly to original research on the study of personality.
- The Educational Department of CAPT offers basic and advanced training worldwide for managers, educators, counselors, psychotherapists, career counselors, psychologists, organizational development consultants, and religious leaders. CAPT has also sponsored and co-sponsored international conferences since 1975.

For further information on the Myers-Briggs Type Indicator or a catalog of books, services and products, you may contact:

Center for Applications of Psychological Type, Inc.
2815 N.W. 13th Street, Suite 401
Gainesville, FL 32609
(800) 777-2278
(352) 375-0160
E-mail: capt@capt.org
Website: http://www.capt.org

About the Authors

Jane A. G. Kise is a freelance writer and management consultant in the fields of strategic planning and team building. She holds a B.A. from Hamline University and an M.B.A. in finance from the University of Minnesota. She is a coauthor of four books on personality type.

Sandra Krebs Hirsh is a management consultant, providing career management and organizational development consultation. She holds graduate degrees in American Studies and Industrial Relations. One of her books on the Myers-Briggs Type Indicator has sold over a million copies. She is much in demand worldwide for her expertise in Human Resources and Organizational Development.